HOW TO HEAL A
GRIEVING HEART

ALSO BY DOREEN VIRTUE AND JAMES VAN PRAAGH

Card Deck (mediumship cards and guidebook)

Talking to Heaven Mediumship Cards

ALSO BY DOREEN VIRTUE

Books/Calendar/Kits/Oracle Board

Angels of Abundance (with Grant Virtue; available August 2014)
Angel Dreams (with Melissa Virtue; available April 2014)
Angel Astrology (with Yasmin Boland; available March 2014)
Angels of Love (with Grant Virtue; available February 2014)
Angel Detox (with Robert Reeves, N.D.; available January 2014)
Assertiveness for Earth Angels
Whispers from Above 2014 Calendar
The Miracles of Archangel Gabriel
Mermaids 101
Flower Therapy (with Robert Reeves)
Mary, Queen of Angels
Saved by an Angel
The Angel Therapy® Handbook
Angel Words (with Grant Virtue)
Archangels 101
The Healing Miracles of Archangel Raphael
The Art of Raw Living Food (with Jenny Ross)
Signs from Above (with Charles Virtue)
The Miracles of Archangel Michael
Angel Numbers 101
Solomon's Angels (a novel)
My Guardian Angel (with Amy Oscar)
Angel Blessings Candle Kit (with Grant Virtue; includes booklet, CD, journal, etc.)
Thank You, Angels! (children's book with Kristina Tracy)
Healing Words from the Angels
How to Hear Your Angels
Realms of the Earth Angels
Fairies 101

Audio/CD Programs

Messages from Your Angels (abridged audio book)
Past-Life Regression with the Angels
Divine Prescriptions
The Romance Angels
Connecting with Your Angels
Manifesting with the Angels
Karma Releasing
Healing Your Appetite, Healing Your Life
Healing with the Angels
Divine Guidance
Chakra Clearing

DVD Program

How to Give an Angel Card Reading

Oracle Cards (divination cards and guidebook)

Past Life Oracle Cards (with Brian Weiss, M.D., available October 2014)
Cherub Angel Cards for Children (available June 2014)
Angels of Abundance Tarot Cards (with Radleigh Valentine; available May 2014)
Archangel Power Tarot Cards (with Radleigh Valentine)
Flower Therapy Oracle Cards (with Robert Reeves)
Indigo Angel Oracle Cards (with Charles Virtue)
Angel Dreams Oracle Cards (with Melissa Virtue)
Mary, Queen of Angels Oracle Cards
Angel Tarot Cards (with Radleigh Valentine and Steve A. Roberts)
The Romance Angels Oracle Cards
Life Purpose Oracle Cards
Archangel Raphael Healing Oracle Cards
Archangel Michael Oracle Cards
Angel Therapy® Oracle Cards
Magical Messages from the Fairies Oracle Cards
Ascended Masters Oracle Cards
Daily Guidance from Your Angels Oracle Cards
Saints & Angels Oracle Cards
Magical Unicorns Oracle Cards
Goddess Guidance Oracle Cards
Archangel Oracle Cards
Magical Mermaids and Dolphins Oracle Cards
Messages from Your Angels Oracle Cards

Healing with the Fairies Oracle Cards
Healing with the Angels Oracle Cards

All of the above are available at your local bookstore, or may be ordered by visiting: Hay House USA: **www.hayhouse.com**®; Hay House Australia: **www .hayhouse.com.au**; Hay House UK: **www.hayhouse.co.uk**; Hay House South Africa: **www.hayhouse.co.za**; Hay House India: **www.hayhouseco.in**

Doreen's website: **www.AngelTherapy.com**

ALSO BY JAMES VAN PRAAGH

Books

Journey of the Soul (available September 2014)
Talking to Heaven
Reaching to Heaven
Healing Grief
Heaven and Earth
Meditations with James Van Praagh
Looking Beyond
Ghosts Among Us
Unfinished Business
Growing Up in Heaven

Card Deck

Journey of the Soul Lesson Cards (available September 2014)

Online Courses

Enhancing Your Intuition
Life After Loss
Mastering Meditation

Downloadable Meditations

Divine Love
Meditation Tools
Soul Discoveries
Spirit Speaks

James's website: **www.vanpraagh.com**

HOW TO HEAL A GRIEVING HEART

Doreen Virtue AND James Van Praagh

HAY HOUSE, INC.
Carlsbad, California • New York City
London • Sydney • Johannesburg
Vancouver • Hong Kong • New Delhi

Library of Congress Control Number: 2013941113

Hardcover ISBN: 978-1-4019-4336-3

16 15 14 13   4 3 2 1

1st edition, October 2013

Printed in China

To my loved ones in heaven.

– DV

To the spirits who have taught me how to love.

– JVP

Contents

INTRODUCTION

Healing Your Grieving Heart

We have both been in your position, with our hearts torn open from the pain of losing someone we loved. We've also supported thousands of grieving people privately and publicly over the 20-plus years we've each been teaching, writing, and counseling. So we know how you feel right now.

We wrote *How to Heal a Grieving Heart* as the book that we wished we'd had during *our* grieving process. Through these pages, we're reaching our hands out to you to walk beside you. We offer you information and guidance, based upon our extensive experiences, with the prayer that it will comfort you.

Grief is a mixture of many emotions, and nothing we can say will bring your loved one physically back.

However, we *can* help you go on with your life. We can also help you better understand why your loved one transitioned, and how you can connect with his or her eternal soul. And we can reassure you that no one ever truly dies, and you will be reunited someday.

Whichever page you open to is what you're meant to read. You don't need to start at the beginning with this book, as it's meant to be a place for you to turn when you need solace. Let the book open where it wants, and allow your mind and heart to also wander freely as you read the message on the page.

You don't need to go through this process alone! Our prayers are with you, and there are wonderful grief support groups online and in person worldwide. Please allow us to help you through this time of transition, accepting our prayers and the healing messages we offer you in this book.

With love,

Doreen and James

Days Can Be Like Butterflies

Some days you can soar and fly, and others you just need to sit back. Be gentle with yourself. You have been through a life-changing experience, and you must take time to relax. The world and life as you know it are different now. Even though you are strong and have always been there for everyone else, now the Universe wants you to be there for yourself. This is a wonderful opportunity that has been given to you—not only to recharge your batteries, but in these still moments, to remind yourself once again just what a beautiful and unique being you are.

A Soul Never Leaves Without Leaving Gifts Behind

What a blessing to have walked this earthly path with another quality soul. The best in you recognized the best in the other person, and together you created unique and special memories that can never die. What wonderful aspects of your being did you share with your loved one? How has his or her beautiful presence impacted your life, and what wonderful gifts did he or she leave with you to assist you in appreciating life differently? You are a better person, and now it is up to you to share those gifts with the world.

God Creates
No Accidents, Just
Divine Timing

When shocking things that appear to be accidents occur, it is impossible for the human part of us to comprehend the fullness of the workings of the Universe. We become mad at God and ask, *How could He do this?* But maybe, somewhere just outside of our human perception, there is a rhythm and a destiny that a soul might have had to fulfill. Perhaps we can eventually transform our shock, anger, and pain into reassurance that just as the stars shine in the sky and the planets revolve around the sun, there is a perfect timing and a rhythm to all things, and one day it will all be revealed to us.

Time Is Just a Placeholder Until You See Each Other Again

Time is truly an illusion, for what is felt in the heart cannot be measured by any clock. But as you live each new day, let it reveal wisdom and insights from your past so that you can have a fuller understanding and appreciation of your tomorrows. As the moments pass, realize that each one is preparing and perfecting you for your reunion . . . so that when that day comes and you step outside of time, you realize the fullness of your love expressed and experienced in its ultimate glory.

Send Healing
Prayers to Heaven

Heaven sends you healing prayers, and you can also send them back to heaven! Pray for your loved ones in Spirit, sending them love and asking for God, Jesus, and the angels to help them as they transition into their afterlife.

LET SILENCE OPEN UP YOUR HEART SO YOU CAN HEAR IT SING

The beginning of all prayer is silence. Honor these moments of self-reflection, and let this journey take you deep within so your soul may speak to you. Only by being in the silence will you truly find the insights you are looking for . . . for your soul has traveled eons of time discovering, experiencing, molding, and creating exactly who you are today. When the voice of the soul begins to unfold, you will witness the true essence of your being.

Words Are Like Powerful Signposts: They Tell the Universe the Direction Our Soul Desires to Go

Many times feelings can only be expressed with the written word. When we take the time to write a letter, a poem, or just a journal entry to our loved ones who have moved on, the purity, intent, and emotions of these words give life to them in the ethers. They not only reinforce to your Spirit family, guides, and angels your love and gratitude, but in an interesting way, they set into motion a clear and precise course in which your soul wishes to proceed in its ongoing journey of healing and insight.

BEING CONNECTED TO NATURE IS BEING IN COMMUNION WITH GOD

Bring yourself to a place in nature that stirs a sense of wonder within you. These are God's natural healing rooms. They are designed to refresh your soul and remind you of your connection to everything in the Universe. In these sacred outdoor spaces, the veil between the worlds is thin, and you can blend into the rhythm of life and commune with all that is inherently holy. Let the sacredness of these spaces open you up to share in the beauty that the entirety of life is offering you.

The Only Constant
in Life Is Change

Just as the ocean ebbs and flows, and the sun rises and sets, every season in your life comes and goes. Life is change, and change is life. It is through change that we are able to clearly measure where we have come from, where we currently are, and where we wish to go next. With change, we gain proper insight and a perspective on our growth. Nothing that *is* will ever stay the same, but hopefully we will find the joy and love within every change we encounter.

THE AMOUNT OF GRIEF
WE FEEL IS EQUAL TO THE
LOVE WE SHARED

Never believe anyone who tells you that there is a finite amount of time you should grieve. There are no rules when it comes to mourning. Grief, like love, is immeasurable. No one loves the same, nor grieves the same. Some people demonstrate their sorrow openly, while others keep it deep within their being. It is a very personal human and spiritual experience. Tears cleanse the soul, and grief validates the love you felt. Rest assured, knowing that your heart and the invisible beings in heaven will assist you in your transformation to a new life filled with ever-growing love and ever-evolving experiences.

A Soul Can Never Die

There is no such thing as death. Death is very much an illusion. A soul can never be harmed, and nothing can put out the light of your being. Many believe that by ending the physical body, they cease to exist. Nothing could be further from the truth. Likewise, there is no condemnation when you cross over, just an awareness of the choices your soul needed to experience. When a soul goes home and is freed from the limitations of the earthly mind, it will be restored to the fullness of its glory and continue to live in the eternal energy of God.

No One Ever Dies Alone

Just as others are here to welcome you into this physical world, your Spirit family, angels, and guides wait for you, assist you, and welcome you back to your spiritual home. They have been part of every earthly moment and have been looking forward to the time when you release your earthly coil. They prepare and plan for your arrival, and all those who you have yearned to be with will be right at your side encouraging you to come closer to their world. They will instill in you an overwhelming peace and joy in your heart, and everything will appear in perfect and natural order. It is then that you will be reunited, and you will realize you have stepped through the veil and are finally back home.

Be Gentle with Yourself

Your heart is raw and open from all of the tears you have cried, and you are extra-sensitive to energy right now. So it is doubly important to spend time only with gentle people whom you can trust and only put yourself in gentle situations. Take time for yourself through naps; with pampering treatments; and by giving yourself permission to just stare into space, reflect, and nurture yourself.

IT'S OKAY TO CRY

Tears are God's gift to cleanse our souls of pain and hurt. Do not hold back the tears or you will dam up strong emotions that will come out in unhealthy ways. Everyone cries, and it is important that you give yourself permission to do so, even at inopportune times. Your tears make you real and accessible and show the world that it is okay to feel and express grief when you are sad. In this way, your tears are a true sign of strength and confidence.

You Can't Change the Past . . . Let It Go!

It is natural to relive the events leading up to your loss, and to wonder if you could have done anything differently. You may even worry that you were at fault. This is called "bargaining," and it is a normal part of grieving. Yet, obsessing over the past does not bring back your loved one, nor does it help anyone or anything. It is a waste of time and energy that could instead be directed toward creating a memorial or perhaps a fund so that losses like yours are not experienced by someone else. Think for a moment of how you want to honor your loved one: with useless regrets or with positive action?

Your Loved One Isn't Gone, Just Shifted

Heaven is not a faraway cloud in the sky; it is parallel to Earth at a higher vibrational frequency. Just like radio and television stations are next to each other on the dial but at different bandwidths, so too is your loved one right next to you. You can feel his or her presence as a vibration. Each person has a unique vibrational frequency, like a snowflake's individuality. So if you think about your loved one, trust that this is a sign that he or she is with you.

BUTTERFLIES,
BIRDS, AND
DRAGONFLIES

Your loved one sends you signs from heaven, and frequently this means winged beings like butterflies, birds, dragonflies, or moths . . . to signify their angel-like flight to heaven. The flying beings are a sign that you are loved, watched over, and protected, *and* that your loved one is safe and happy in heaven. There may even be a specific type of bird or butterfly that was your loved one's favorite, and seeing it lets you know without a doubt of his or her enduring presence and love.

Songs of Love

When you hear a special song that reminds you of your loved one, allow yourself time to stop, close your eyes, and breathe. Music, being nonphysical, acts as a bridge between heaven and Earth. So songs are sent to you as messages of love. If one moves you to cry, it is best to let the tears flow . . . even if it is inconvenient or embarrassing to show your emotions. Music opens the heart so that you can feel heaven's love pouring out to you, helping reassure you that your love is always alive.

"TOGETHER WE WILL GET THROUGH THIS"

From their side of life, the Spirit people come close to you and share every one of your hopes, wishes, and dreams. They clearly hear your thoughts and will try to influence you in ways that are for your highest good. They will walk every step with you, attempting to let you know that life is not over . . . just different. They will bring into your life every possible situation they can in order to remind you that they are with you and that no one is alone.

There Is No Pain in Death

As humans we must begin to understand that death itself is not to be feared. The transition when a soul actually leaves the physical vessel is indeed painless. This has been proved via countless near-death experiences. There is an immediate sense of being free. The soul no longer experiences the physical discomforts that he or she had lived with toward the end. Every death is an extremely joyful birth into a higher dimension of awareness and being.

Releasing the Pain

Being part of this human experience and learning in this schoolroom called "Earth" is full of extremely hard human lessons. Grief is one of the hardest. Losing someone presents us with challenges and hurt. But as a soul, we must never forget that these difficult lessons are also the ones through which we evolve spiritually. The pain does not define you; it is just a validation of your love. Never suppress it, for you need to go through this process in order to bring about the fullness of the experience.

DISBELIEF AND SHOCK

You are probably feeling like a stranger in a strange land. Your entire world seems upside down, and no one can put it back to "normal." You may even feel as if you and your life have become "robotic," just going through the motions. Disbelief and shock go in tandem. Because we are so used to the people in our lives and living out old patterns, when something changes, we do not want to believe it. Sometimes we will even remain in denial for a while in order not to make this new situation real. All these reactions are normal. Remember to take each day as it comes, knowing you are still sensitive to the changed circumstances.

After a Loss, You Know Your True Priorities

By losing someone, we are forced to recalibrate our lives and remember what is important to us and what is not. Use this experience to look around your world and see who supports you in it and who does not. Is there something in your life you have always wanted to accomplish but still never have? This is a time to begin new things. With these newfound insights, it creates a shift in our awareness, reminding us that we are merely borrowing time on this earth and that one day we will go back home. It is important to know that the amount of love we have left behind for others is all that matters.

Anger Is Part of Being Human

Feeling powerless and out of control is quite common when we go through a loss. It is because death is something we cannot control, and we wish we could have done something to forestall its inevitability. Many times we direct our anger to those who we feel might have prevented this unwelcome event from occurring—even God! We also get angry at ourselves, thinking we could have stopped this if only *we* had done something. The last thing your loved one would want is for you to direct anger at yourself.

Confusion Is Normal

Nothing makes sense and you cannot think clearly, because this event has so suddenly rocked you. No, you are not going crazy. Everyone who goes through a devastating loss experiences this. There may be loss of memory, loss of time, even the complete confusion of not knowing where you are! This will slowly pass as the days and months go by, but at the beginning it seems "all or nothing." It is important to also remember that you are not in this alone. Every day there are thousands of others who are having the exact same experience you are. You may even speak to them and ask for a helping hand, and eventually a sense of normalcy will come back into your life.

GRIEF IS AN UNCONTROLLABLE RIDE

The emotions of grief can be like riding a roller coaster: you are not sure when the turn is coming or how far you will fall. It is sudden and scary, and you feel completely out of control. One moment you might be smiling, and the next you are uncontrollably crying. Unfortunately, grief by its very nature is "out of control" and filled with surprise emotions and reactions that arise at any time. The most important thing to remember is that you are strong, and eventually this ride to will come to a halt.

"I Never Knew
I Could Be This Sad"

Sadness is one of the strongest emotions felt after a loss. The journey of sadness can bring us to the lowest of lows and the very depths of despair. We feel as if we cannot get out, and no one can share it with us. We feel isolated. We realize that we will no longer see our loved one again, nor share in life's tender moments. We question our own mortality and keep on asking *Why?* Throughout the sorrow we must also realize that we are still alive and therefore have a purpose to serve. Honor your loved one by making a promise to fulfill your life purpose and replace your sadness with that which brings you happiness and joy.

PEOPLE SAY THE STRANGEST THINGS

The most unpopular subject for most people is death. It makes them feel uncomfortable, because most fear it. The majority will say they understand what you are going through, but truly they do not fully. In an attempt to make you feel better, people may make some very insensitive remarks. Even though what they said was inappropriate, they are sincerely attempting to help you, because they want nothing but for you to be okay and for everything to return back to normal. Just know that their motivation comes from a place of love. Even when people love you, sometimes they cannot help acting strange.

"I Am Too Sensitive . . . I Can't Take It"

During this grieving process, you may find that you just do not think you can take it anymore! Every reaction and situation seems to be magnified. Nothing is like it used to be. You are ultrasensitive and completely "on guard" against anyone who comes into your space and makes an attempt to alter it. This is normal. You need a sense of comfort and some familiarity. Indulge in activities you love and that bring a sense of control back to your life.

Maybe It Is Time to Learn How to Ask for Help

Grief many times forces us to remember that it is always good to ask for help. Sometimes two are better than one. Even if all it is, is for someone to listen to you, that will help. Never feel as if you have to do this alone, because you do *not.* Friends are always willing to be there, but sometimes you might need to guide them into the conversation. In doing so, you will find that your friendships become stronger. Remember that it is giving the other person an opportunity to grow from and share this experience as well.

What You Think Is the End Is Merely the Beginning

The biggest illusion of this world is death. We think our loved ones are gone, and physically they may be, but spiritually they have just begun their journey and are lighter, more expansive, and more receptive than ever witnessed here. Now they can assist us by influencing us to do what is best for our soul nature. By their movement from our world, it forces us to ask the big life questions, and just by inquiring, we may find that life takes us down an enlightened road of understanding, leading to insights we never thought possible before.

The Soul's True Nature Is Not of the Earth . . .

We are first and foremost spiritual beings having a physical experience. As souls visiting this earth, we make an attempt to utilize our spiritual heritage in human experiences. Part of our mission is to remember the soul's language of intuition. With this recognition, we open the door to the light of the Divine Source, and this energy will transform every component of our lives. By getting more in tune with our soul nature, we are better equipped to understand the hurdles this world will throw at us.

In Order to Stand Up Straight, You Must Stumble Sometimes

Nothing in life is perfect, not even death. It comes to us at the most inconvenient times and can certainly wreak havoc in our worlds. Most times it will emotionally push us over the edge, and we lose all sense of stability. Every new situation is a learning experience; and slowly, carefully, we must move through it. The same may be said about grief. It knocks us down as we lose our footing, but eventually we will stand up again to face a new life.

The Harder Challenges Are, the More We Have to Fight to Meet Them

At first grief is a harrowing experience. Since our world is immediately turned upside down, we seem to be grasping at anything to get us through. When we are in the darkest moments of life, it seems that we are forced to go within to the core of our being and uncover a strength we have yet to discover. Within you there is a key for you to unlock even the hardest parts of the human drama. Within your heart sit lifetimes of soul experiences for you to draw upon when the most difficult challenges of life are being presented to you.

Healing Mementos

You may find comfort by holding a memento that reminds you of your loved one. Perhaps an item of clothing with the person's unique fragrance and energy, or an object that you bought together. You may even sleep with these items to feel closer to your loved one. While the memento will not bring your loved one back physically, it does help you connect with the eternal love and bond that you will always share with each other.

Dance with Your Loved One

Play your favorite music, close your eyes, and dance with your loved one! You'll feel his or her presence close to you, as you both enjoy the opportunity to join through the healing bridge of music.

HOLIDAYS CAN
STILL BE SPECIAL

Your loved one will still be present for all holidays and special occasions, and you can make the day even more magical by honoring his or her life and memory. For example, wrap a box that is filled with love and prayers, and put it under the Christmas tree. You can ceremoniously unwrap it "together," and you will feel your loved one's appreciation. Other ideas: save a chair at a graduation or wedding, and celebrate the person's birthday.

When You Least Expect It . . .

. . . something will re-
mind you of your loved
one in heaven. You may
see his or her name on
an e-mail, or watch a
movie on TV that you
both enjoyed together.
Know that these are lov-
ing signs from heaven.

WHAT DID YOU PLAN TO DO TOGETHER?

Did you both dream of going on a Mediterranean cruise? Did you talk about listening to that French-language-course recording that you purchased together? Did you plan to organize your family photos? These activities can still be pursued, as a way to share your love in a whole new way. Your life continues, and your loved one would want you to fill your heart with the joy of taking action toward your dreams. Whether you invite another good friend on the cruise or go by yourself, for example, know that your loved one will be accompanying you.

Honoring Your Loved Ones

Your friends and family in heaven appreciate you honoring them in charitable ways. When you plant a tree, name a star, give a donation, or start a foundation in their honor, you give the gift of allowing their memory and energy to live on and help others.

CREATIVE HEALING

You may feel confused by all the mixed emotions from your loss, including anger, bewilderment, shock, guilt, and fear. These emotions are powerful energies that need an outlet so that they do not stay inside of you and stew in unhealthy ways. One outlet to release pent-up emotions is through creative expression, such as writing and journaling, crafts, painting, poetry, music, dance, and flower arranging. Although you may not feel like you are in an artistic mood, remember that a lot of masterpieces were created when artists poured their angst and sorrow into their creations.

Dealing with Family Members

Everyone deals with grief differently, and sometimes grieving people act in hurtful ways because they *are* hurt. Your own family members may begin quarreling over inheritances, estate items, and funeral arrangements. Before getting involved in arguments or taking sides, ask yourself how much each topic really matters to you. You may realize that anger is a reaction to grief, and it is not worth magnifying the loss in the family with divisions and arguments.

TAKE A
BREAK FROM
SADNESS

At first, hearing songs that remind you of your loved one can help you feel closer. The same is true with gazing at photos and other memorabilia. But at some point, these sentimental items may put you on a sadness overload ... and that is when you will know it is time to take a break from sorrow. At those moments, give yourself permission to put the photos away (even just temporarily) and focus upon visuals that uplift your heart and soul. You can always bring the mementos out later when you are feeling stronger and more healed.

Plant and Grow
Your Love

Planting a tree, flowers, or a garden in honor of your loved one is a special way to commemorate your relationship. Gardening in itself is therapeutic, and you can more clearly feel and hear your loved one's presence and messages when you are outside in nature.

You Don't Have to Do This Alone

There are online and in-person grief support and recovery groups available to help you. If you feel like you cannot go on with your life, please reach out to professionals and those who have experienced big losses like yours. They understand. They care. They are there for you.

Loss Changes Everything

Sometimes it takes a tragedy to open our hearts to what really matters in life. Your grief will have you questioning *everything*, and you may be tempted to make drastic life changes. It is healthy to reevaluate, as loss helps us remember our true priorities. However, watch out for impulsive and reckless decisions that might be influenced by your intense grief. If you still feel like making huge changes two or three months from now, you will know that your feelings are grounded and realistic.

GIVE UP GUILT

It is normal to feel guilt over a loved one's passing, as you wonder what you might have done differently. You may also feel guilty about some of the thoughts and emotions you are experiencing. For example, you may feel anger at the person for leaving you, or for not taking better care of his or her health . . . and these feelings may lead to guilt if you are uncomfortable with being mad at someone in heaven. Please know that it is perfectly normal and understandable to adjust to your new situation with resistance and resentment. However, try not to hold these powerful emotions inside. Talk with heaven about all of your feelings, and trust that whatever you feel is part of your healing experience.

The Angels Love You

You have guardian angels with you right now who love you unconditionally. These are celestial beings assigned to each of us by our Creator. You can talk to your angels about *anything*, and they will not judge you in any way. The angels can offer assistance with your emotions, sleep, health, and every aspect of your loss. However, because of the Law of Free Will, they can only help if you ask. It does not matter *how* you ask, but only that you do so. The angels work with the infinite Divine wisdom to enact wonderful solutions, so you need not worry about how your requests will be answered. Just ask for help, and trust that God and the angels will assist you in a Divinely perfect way.

Sleeping
and Healing

Loss affects sleep patterns, and you may wonder if you will ever again get a good night's rest. *You will.* Right after a loss, it is normal to awaken frequently or to be plagued by frightening dreams. This is your unconscious mind's healing process, where it releases deep-seated fears about death, abandonment, and loss. Avoid the temptation to medicate yourself in order to sleep, as that will not help you achieve the restfulness and peace you are seeking. A healthful lifestyle and facing your fears while awake (with the help of a counselor, if possible) will allow you to get a good night's sleep that is restorative and healing.

Scary Thoughts

When you lose someone who means the world to you, you may not want to continue on without that person. You may get frightening thoughts of joining your loved one in heaven. Having these thoughts occasionally is normal, but if you ever find yourself making plans to harm yourself . . . stop, and call immediately for professional help. Your life purpose is not over yet, and your family needs you. When it is your time to go, you *will* rejoin all your loved ones in heaven and see them again. Promise!

HONOR YOUR ENERGY LEVELS

Grief is one of the most draining conditions to experience, so it is no wonder that you are feeling tired a lot. If your enthusiasm is gone and you are having difficulty getting out of bed, you are not alone. These are effects of losing someone who means so much to you. You may feel like hiding in bed so you will not have to face another day alone. Honor these feelings, and do not feel guilty for taking a day or two to rest. However, also know that you can feel a lot better by making yourself take a shower, get dressed, and leave the house. Although you may not yet be ready to face a social event, you will feel uplifted by driving to the local park and feeding the birds or getting some sunshine and fresh air.

Focus and Concentration

The confusion you feel is part of the reorganization process of grieving. You are probably struggling with forgetfulness and are having difficulty following through on simple plans. So, take your time in doing everything, even if it feels as if you are moving in slow motion. Write lists to help you remember, and place items that you need to take with you near the front door. Always put your car keys, checkbook, and glasses in the same places so you can easily find them. And remember that all of this is a temporary reaction to a very serious life change you are experiencing. So have compassion for yourself if you are forgetful, and know that you are doing the best you can.

This Loss May Bring Up Other Losses

Any unhealed grief from previous losses is likely to be resurrected once again by this one. This compounds and intensifies the feelings you are experiencing. Your emotions may roller-coaster and have a mind of their own. This signifies that it is time, once and for all, to deal with your feelings over the major losses in your life. It is a lot like finally cleaning out your closet or garage—not a fun task, but one that is necessary to keep order. Fortunately, there are lots of qualified grief counselors who can hold your hand during the process. Or if you are lucky enough to have a trusted friend who knows the path of healing from grief, you have an angel by your side to help you.

When We Avoid Grief,
We Avoid Life

Loss is very much a part of life, and no one is immune to its devastation and emotional upheavals. The best thing you can do for yourself is to be present with your grief and try to move through every aspect of it. As painful as it seems right now, in the future you will be able to look back and understand how the experience has also given you some positive insights. When we avoid the pain of grief, we find that it impacts our lives in ways we never imagined it would.

LIVE IN LOVE,
NOT FEAR

When we are released from the body, we immediately feel the Universal love within every particle of life. We understand how our fears in the lifetime limited our perspectives and the fullness of our experience. Let your loss remind you that you are an eternal being of love and you truly have nothing to fear.

Create Some Beautiful Thoughts, for the Spirits Are Watching

We are constantly creating our reality with our thoughts. No one sees this more than our loved ones in the Spirit world. Remember that they are always aware of what you are creating with your thoughts . . . so be proud of the thoughts you send into the Spirit world.

Open Your Eyes to the Light of Spirit

During the day, try to focus your eyes on something that is beautiful in your world. It could be a flower, a landscape, a cloud formation—anything related to nature—and just try for a few moments to become aware of your loved one standing next to you in a golden light. The best part of this person sees the best part of you.

Don't Wait to Grieve . . . Let It Out

It is very important for your future well-being to allow yourself to grieve immediately when your loss is fresh. But do not try to rush through it either. Let it flow; move through at your own pace. You should never be worried what others might think of you crying or being upset; this is none of your concern, and grieving is an extremely personal and healthy experience.

Love Is Where
the Heart Is

The memories you and your loved one created in life now live on in your heart for all time. Memories stay with you forever; they can never go away! They are always there for you to enjoy, so remember and relive those wonderful, happy, and unique moments you shared.

LET THIS BE YOUR OPPORTUNITY TO CHANGE

Each day life brings along moments for us to reflect, look inside, and choose if we want to continue living the same way . . . or make the necessary changes to enrich our lives upon this earth. Look closely at the opportunities this experience of loss affords you, and take advantage of them. You will never have a chance to be in this particular space again.

Try to Find a Blessing in Every Burden

You have heard the expression "Every cloud has a silver lining." It is very true. For every experience that seems "negative" or sad, there is always a polar opposite available within the same experience. Many times our souls are being tested to see if we can find the hidden blessings.

Forgiveness Is Always Available

Many times when we lose someone, we find we are forced to forgive the person, others, or even the circumstances in which he or she left. Forgiveness is really a gift you give yourself . . . for in this act, you release resentments and thoughts of revenge. Of course, you may never *forget* the experience, but at least by forgiving, it will not have a hold on you, and you can begin to focus on more positive aspects of your life.

BE OPEN TO RECEIVING

In times of loss, it may be important to remember that others can be a vital part of your healing. Let them assist you, share with you, and take care of you. Many times it is through others' compassion and caring that the journey of grief becomes easier to understand and move through. The experience of loss is shared by everyone, so you never know who might be able to offer the exact words you need to hear to lighten your heart.

A Peaceful Mind Is a Happy Mind

Every day we are bombarded by outside stimuli. Today there are way too many things that consume our thoughts. The more things we worry about, the less peace of mind we possess. A mind at peace keeps you calm, happy, and more productive. In this time, try as best you can to not "think" so much. Unplug from phones, e-mails, and even talking at length. Bring your mind into a state of ease and restfulness.

Your Spirit Family Is Right Next to You

Just because your loved one has moved on to the higher dimension does not mean he or she has forgotten about you and is uninterested in your life. It is just the opposite. Via the Spirit body, the person is able to travel with you, just by using his or her thoughts. Your loved one's awareness of you and your desires is much more amplified, and he or she will continue to share life with you, just in a different way.

EARTH IS THE SOUL'S SCHOOLROOM

Earth is just one of many schools our souls can choose to come back to in order to learn various spiritual-growth lessons. Forgiveness, compassion, and of course, love can be some of the most difficult lessons to fully comprehend and discover. But once we do understand them, we will go to the head of the class. If there were no challenges in the name of growth, it would defeat the whole reason for going to school in the first place.

Karma Is Not a Punishment

Unfortunately, the term *karma* has taken on a negative connotation, and there is little understanding of its true meaning. Karma is really the awareness that we are personally responsible for what we create and put out to the Universe. It is a direct result of our thoughts and actions. Think of it as "energy," with the understanding that you will experience exactly the same energy you put forth. Thus, if you project love, you get back love. So it is good or bad, depending on how *you* choose to use it.

SPIRITS MAKE UP
YOUR DREAMS

One of the most common methods spirits will use to let us know that they are still with us is by appearing in our dreams. These dreams are very different from our usual ones. They often appear to be extremely "real" to us emotionally and physically . . . and that is because they *are!* Our own Spirit bodies will "meet up" with our loved ones during the sleep state on the Spirit side of life. Most times the conscious mind does not remember, but when it does, we are reminded of how strong our loving bonds still are.

You're Never Quite Ready

Whether your loss occurred suddenly, or was expected after a long illness, you are never really ready to say good-bye to your loved one's physical presence. And even if you know that the person is in a better place and is out of pain, it is still difficult to realize that you are unable to pick up the telephone and call whenever you wish. Now, you have to wait to see him or her again at the end of your natural life. The good news, though, is that your loved one does see you and visits you frequently in your dreams, when you need help, and while you are engaged in activities that you two once shared. Be gentle with your fragile feelings, and know that what you are experiencing is part of the healing process.

Don't Let Yourself Obsess

During the grieving process, you may find yourself staring off into space, lost in thoughts about your loved one in heaven. You may obsessively worry whether your loved one suffered during his or her passing. Your mind tries to hunt down every possible clue, in search of the truth. Unfortunately, obsessing does not physically bring back your loved one or give you the peace of mind you are seeking. Obsessing is a downward spiral that only attracts more negativity. Your loved one in heaven would not want you to focus upon the negative. Rather, he or she would want you to enjoy your life as much as possible. So, please give your cares, concerns, and worries to God and the angels through prayer: *"Dear God, please help me release my fears and worries, and honor my loved one by living my life to the fullest."*

"I Should Have . . ." and Other Regrets

Please do not beat yourself up mentally, berating yourself for something you think you should have done. Yes, you probably could have visited more, spoken up, said "I love you," driven that day, or taken a whole host of other actions. But regrets will not bring back your loved one. Instead, see your regrets as life lessons never to be repeated. Realize that you were doing the best you could at each moment, based upon what you knew at the time. And direct your regrets in positive ways, such as teaching others what you now know.

Filling the Emptiness

If your heart feels empty, like no one or nothing else can take the place of your loved one, then you have two choices: live with the emptiness, or take action steps to fill the void in new ways. Hopefully, you will choose the second option, because you have many years left and you may as well enjoy your time. Misery does not honor your loved one; happiness does! So, start accepting invitations to parties, social clubs, and activities, even if you have to make yourself join in. Your heart will soon be filled with new forms of love.

Your Routines Will Go On . . .

All those routines that you and your loved one shared are altered now. You may be avoiding those routines, doing them alone in a bewildered daze, or looking for other companionship. Know that your loved one in heaven *does* still join with you for special activities, in new nonphysical ways.

WHEN YOU CAN'T
FEEL YOUR LOVED
ONE'S PRESENCE

You hear and read about other people's encounters with their departed loved ones, and you wonder: *Where is mine?* If you have not felt this energetic presence, please do not despair. It does not mean you have been abandoned or are unloved. Usually, it signifies that your loved one is involved in much-needed self-care. Each person has a different heavenly path for his or her soul's growth. For instance, those who didn't believe in life after death may be shocked when their consciousness survives. They have to rest in the afterlife plane while they adjust to the fact that their souls live on. Other people who have had traumatic deaths need caretaking in heaven before they are strong enough to make visits to family and friends. And still others who are highly evolved ascend above the earth plane and are not physically palpable. You can more easily feel your loved one's presence by keeping your feeling senses alive and awake, which means avoiding numbing yourself with addictions or stuffing down feelings. In time, you will both adjust to feeling each other's presence across the veil.

Flickering Lights and Other "Hello's"

Your loved one will learn how to interact with the physical world to send you signs. This includes intercepting electronic signals and saying, "Hello, I'm here and I love you!" by flickering the lights and the screen of your television set. The soul may also send greetings through the telephone, including a call with his or her caller identification. Heaven has gotten high-tech in its ability to send you loving messages and signs!

When the Pain Is Unbearable...

As the reality of your loved one's passing sinks in, you may hurt so much that you wonder how you will survive. Sweetheart, you will—and you must—survive. Many are counting on you now. You have an inner strength that comes straight from God and heaven. Call upon this strength now. Reach deep into your core, pull up your power, and return to living the life that is part of your purpose and calling. Vow to help others who are experiencing the same thing as you, and apply the lessons from your painful experiences in order to help others.

"Why Didn't God Answer My Prayers?"

You prayed and you prayed for your loved one to live . . . and yet he or she died anyway. When a person's life is in balance, the angels offer him or her the choice to return home to heaven or stay in the physical body. And while it may seem unbelievable that someone would *choose* to go to heaven, staying in his or her physical body may have been an even more painful option for your loved one. For instance, this person may have been sparing you the work involved in providing his or her health care, or may have seen how his or her passing awakened your spiritual growth. God cannot interfere with an individual's freewill choices, and we all need to pray for the grace and acceptance that our loved ones made a decision that they felt was best.

Your Dogs and Cats Know!

If your dog is barking at a blank wall, or your cat is hissing and scurrying away out of the blue, it is because animals are natural mediums who can sense the presence of your departed loved ones. To your pets, their energy is the same as a physical presence, so your dog will bark at a visitor or wag his tail to greet a familiar person. Our pets know that our souls are eternally alive.

WRITE A LETTER TO HEAVEN

All of heaven can hear your thoughts and sense your feelings, but it is also helpful for your healing to organize and pour out your thoughts in a letter. You can write it longhand with pen and paper, or on your computer. You can ask heaven any question you like, and you will always receive answers that you will "hear" as thoughts, feelings, visions, signs, or words in your mind.

Even When You Don't Feel Sociable . . .

Life is for the living, and that means spending time with other living people, even if you must force yourself to become sociable again. Through the grieving process, you quickly discover who your true friends are, and who offers comfort and support. These are the folks to spend time with, as they will accept that you might not be yet "yourself." They will love you, even if you are grumpy or depressed because of your grieving process.

Eating Healthfully Helps!

How have you been eating lately? How would your loved one feel about your diet? Your body is a gift, and it is the only one you have for your entire life. Your loved one in heaven wants you to take excellent care of your body, and that means paying attention to proper nutrition. So make the time to shop for some organic and unprocessed foods at your local health-food store, healthy restaurant, or farmers' market. Your loved one will smile in heaven as you take good care of yourself!

Sometimes It's Just a Matter of Getting Dressed

Your home reflects your mood. So one way to elevate your mood is to open your curtains and let light in. If the weather allows, open the windows and get some fresh air circulating to clear stale heaviness out of your home. Get out of bed, take a shower, and get dressed. It is the simple action steps that make a huge positive difference.

Don't Take This Loss Personally

You were not abandoned by your loved one. He or she had a reason for leaving, according to Divine timing, and it had nothing to do with you. Yes, his or her passing hurt you terribly and created a void and additional burdens for you to carry. But please know that heaven always sends healing and assistance in the form of miracles and helpful humans. Be open to receiving help.

On Every Important Occasion . . .

Your loved ones will attend every important function with you, such as weddings, graduations, births, and family gatherings. Be sure to acknowledge their spiritual presence and include them in the festivities, even if it is just a silent conversation that you have within your mind during the event.

"Why Did This Happen?"

In time, all of your questions about your loved one's passing will be answered. Someday soon, you will know the truth. In the meantime, allow yourself to be at peace with the uncertainty. It is okay for you to not understand.

EVERYONE LOVES TO HELP

Your loved ones in heaven are honored when you ask for their aid. It is best to consult as high up as possible, such as with God or Jesus, when making important life decisions. But if Aunt Ruth made world-class chocolate-chip cookies, there is nothing wrong with asking her to oversee your baking. Same with Dad's magical ability to fix cars, and Sis's green thumb in the garden. Each person—living and departed—has a special knack for something, and everyone is happy to help . . . even from heaven!

"TAKE ME, TOO!"

Sometimes people react to grief by asking God to take them, too. This is a normal reaction and comes out of anger, shock, and a sense of unfairness. Realize that your loved one is still with you and may have to complete his or her soul's mission from the other side of life, just as you must on this one. Every soul has a time to come into this world and a time to leave.

Looks Like a Spa Day!

Now is a perfect time for you to change up your routine and do something that is all about *you!* Go to the spa and get a massage or a facial. Treat yourself to a lovely day to nurture yourself. You may also find that going to buy a new outfit will lift you up and give you a little bit of joy.

Take a Trip

Now may be a great time to take that trip you have always wanted to go on but have procrastinated about. If you do not jump into things, "life" tends to happen and get in the way. Take a deep breath and pick a place you have always wanted to visit, and make the efforts necessary to turn your wish into a reality. It will give your heart a holiday and allow you time to be with your new self.

THE BLAME GAME

When a loved one passes at a time or under circumstances that seem unnatural, self-inflicted, or too soon, one of the first reactions we may have is to blame ourselves. We think, *If only I had said this or done that, this would not have happened.* This is not true. Every soul has a journey and lessons to learn. No one can live another's life for him or her, and at the time you made the perfect choice. Do not be hard on yourself; you did the best you could have.

Why Aren't
Others Sad, Too?

When we are in the midst of our grief and are so upset, we often will wonder why others cannot feel what we do, and question how they could go about their normal lives when something this devastating has happened. Everyone has a different relationship with a loved one and will express the loss differently. Just know that your loved one in Spirit knows of your sadness and feels *your* love.

Pennies from Heaven

Our loved ones in Spirit are so excited to let us know that they are "alive" and with us that they will try many ways to come through in order for us to take notice of them. One of the most common methods is that they are able to materialize coins where you are likely to find them. So, next time you keep on seeing coins in the strangest of places, know that your loved one is once again saying "hello!"

Your Loves Ones Are "Photogenic"

How exciting! One way your loved ones may attempt to come through to you is in the form of energy in photographs, known as *orbs*. These are concentrated energy structures your loved ones project onto your camera, just so that you know they are with you. Next time you feel them come to you . . . snap a photo and see if their bright light appears.

Reliving Memories

A wonderful method for you to remember your loved one and honor him or her at the same time is to go through all of your shared photos and former videos, and put your creativity in high gear. Make a DVD capturing the many moments you have spent together. This way you have a place to go when you want to relive the beautiful memories you created.

Reorganize Your Life

When your mind is full and you feel completely out of control, one of the best methods to feel better is to reorganize and clean out your closet, office, and environment. You will find that when you do this, you soon realize that you are in control of many aspects of your world. By cleaning and moving things out, you also create more room for new things to come in. (Not to mention that spirits love a clean, fun atmosphere they can share with you!)

TRIBUTES TO YOUR LOVED ONES

Your loved ones are completely aware of, and in tune with, your thoughts. Therefore they are always moved by the little acts of kindness when you create and share wonderful mementos of their lives, such as scrapbooks, photo albums, songs, and memorial videos—all in their honor.

Volunteer Work

Many who are grieving find that the painful process is made a little bit easier when they are in service to others in need. So perhaps consider volunteering with a charitable organization. You can ease your heart and help others all at the same time.

A Memorial Scholarship

The Spirit people, especially those who pass young, always want to give others on Earth the best chance at being all they can be. Many times family members and friends will set up a scholarship or award program in the name of their loved one in heaven, who receives such joy knowing that through his or her passage, another person's life experience on Earth was bettered.

Make an Appointment

Since the Spirit world shares our lives with us, the departed constantly want to reassure us that they are in a very good and loving space. The only problem might be that you are not able to hear them. So, if you want to set aside a specific time of the day or night to connect with them, you should do so. Just make sure it is the same time every day, and of course, keep the appointment! When the time comes, have a pad and pen ready, close your eyes, take a few deep breaths, and listen to what they have to share.

"I Did Not Die in Vain"

Whenever a loved one passes away from this world, we ask, *Why?* It is hard to understand the timing of any passing. But as days, months, and years go by, this experience will eventually be used in order to help another person going through a similar situation. Nothing in life should ever be taken for granted.

HEALING YOUR WOUNDS

You are a powerful, spiritual being who can accomplish anything you set your mind to. Always remember that a broken heart is a heart made larger than before. Your emotional wounds will slowly evolve into something else. Now, in your imagination bring yourself to a place of perfect healing in body, mind, and spirit. Remember that out of the darkness the light will always shine to show you the way.

About the Authors

Doreen Virtue holds B.A., M.A., and Ph.D. degrees in counseling psychology. As a former psychotherapist, she conducted traditional grief counseling, especially as it pertained to her clients' addiction recovery. Doreen has also written about healing from grief in her books *The Lightworker's Way, How to Hear Your Angels,* and *The Angel Therapy Handbook,* and she and James have published a card deck called *Talking to Heaven Mediumship Cards* as a companion to this book.

Doreen has appeared on *Oprah, CNN, The View,* and other television and radio programs, and writes regular columns for *Woman's World* magazine. Her products are available in most languages worldwide, on Kindle and other eBook platforms, and as iTunes apps.

For more information on Doreen and the workshops she presents, please visit: www.AngelTherapy.com. You can listen to Doreen's live weekly radio show, and call her for a reading, by visiting HayHouseRadio.com®.

ANGEL THERAPY®

❦ ❦ ❦

James Van Praagh is an internationally renowned #1 *New York Times* best-selling author. He has written extensively about life after death, Spirit communication, grief, and healing; and his messages have brought solace, peace, and spiritual insights to millions, changing their views on both life and death.

James introduced the world to mediumship on the NBC daytime television show *The Other Side* in 1994. Since then, he has appeared on nearly every national radio and television program, including *Oprah, Larry King Live, Dr. Phil,* A&E's *Biography, Nightline, Unsolved Mysteries, The View, The Joy Behar Show,* the *Today* show, *Dr. Drew's Lifechangers, Chelsea Lately, Coast to Coast,* and many more. His international reach expanded even further when he hosted his very own daytime talk show, *Beyond with James Van Praagh.*

James is also a successful producer in network television. His credits include one of the most-viewed miniseries in CBS history, *Living with the Dead,* starring Ted Danson, portraying James in a biography of his life; and *The Dead Will Tell,* starring Eva Longoria. In addition, he co-created and produced the highly successful series *The Ghost Whisperer,* starring Jennifer Love Hewitt.

James teaches workshops and classes and performs mediumship demonstrations throughout the world. For more information, please visit his website: www .vanpraagh.com.

Grief Support

You can find kind and compassionate support from people who understand at a grief support group. Many are free or low cost. Contact a local hospice provider to obtain a list of recommended groups in your area. You can also find free support online at: www.griefnet.org.

Hay House Titles of Related Interest

YOU CAN HEAL YOUR LIFE, the movie, starring
Louise L. Hay & Friends (available as a 1-DVD
program and an expanded 2-DVD set)
Watch the trailer at: www.LouiseHayMovie.com

THE SHIFT, the movie, starring Dr. Wayne W. Dyer
(available as a 1-DVD program and an expanded 2-DVD set)
Watch the trailer at: www.DyerMovie.com

TUNE IN: Follow Your Intuition from Fear to Flow,
by Sonia Choquette

LOVE HAS FORGOTTEN NO ONE: The Answer to Life,
by Gary R. Renard

*HEART OF THE MATTER: A Simple Guide to Discovering
Gifts in Strange Wrapping Paper,*
by Dr. Darren R. Weissman and Cate Montana, M.A.

*NO STORM LASTS FOREVER: Transforming
Suffering into Insight,* by Dr. Terry A. Gordon

*THROUGH THE EYES OF ANOTHER: A Medium's Guide
to Creating Heaven on Earth by Encountering Your Life
Review Now,* by Karen Noe

*WISHES FOR THE GRIEVING AND HEALING HEART:
Why the Dragonfly Cries,* by Tricia LaVoice

All of the above are available at your local bookstore,
or may be ordered by contacting Hay House (see next page).

We hope you enjoyed this Hay House Lifestyles book. If you'd like to receive our online catalog featuring additional information on Hay House books and products, or if you'd like to find out more about the Hay Foundation, please contact:

Hay House, Inc.
P.O. Box 5100,
Carlsbad, CA 92018-5100

(760) 431-7695 or (800) 654-5126
(760) 431-6948 (fax) or (800) 650-5115 (fax)
www.hayhouse.com® • www.hayfoundation.org

Published and distributed in Australia by: Hay House Australia Pty. Ltd., 18/36 Ralph St., Alexandria NSW 2015 • *Phone:* 612-9669-4299 • *Fax:* 612-9669-4144 • www.hayhouse.com.au

Published and distributed in the United Kingdom by: Hay House UK, Ltd., Astley House, 33 Notting Hill Gate, London W11 3JQ *Phone:* 44-20-3675-2450 • *Fax:* 44-20-3675-2451 www.hayhouse.co.uk

Published and distributed in the Republic of South Africa by: Hay House SA (Pty), Ltd., P.O. Box 990, Witkoppen 2068 *Phone/Fax:* 27-11-467-8904 • www.hayhouse.co.za

Published in India by: Hay House Publishers India, Muskaan Complex, Plot No. 3, B-2, Vasant Kunj, New Delhi 110 070 • *Phone:* 91-11-4176-1620 • *Fax:* 91-11-4176-1630 • www.hayhouse.co.in

Distributed in Canada by: Raincoast, 9050 Shaughnessy St., Vancouver, B.C. V6P 6E5 • *Phone:* (604) 323-7100 *Fax:* (604) 323-2600 • www.raincoast.com

Take Your Soul on a Vacation

Visit www.HealYourLife.com® to regroup, recharge, and reconnect with your own magnificence.

Featuring blogs, mind-body-spirit news, and life-changing wisdom from Louise Hay and friends.

Visit www.HealYourLife.com today!

Free e-newsletters from Hay House, the Ultimate Resource for Inspiration

Be the first to know about Hay House's dollar deals, free downloads, special offers, affirmation cards, giveaways, contests, and more!

 Get exclusive excerpts from our latest releases and videos from **Hay House Present Moments**.

 Enjoy uplifting personal stories, how-to articles, and healing advice, along with videos and empowering quotes, within **Heal Your Life**.

 Have an inspirational story to tell and a passion for writing? Sharpen your writing skills with insider tips from **Your Writing Life**.

Sign Up Now!

Get inspired, educate yourself, get a complimentary gift, and share the wisdom!

http://www.hayhouse.com/newsletters.php

Visit www.hayhouse.com to sign up today!

 HAY HOUSE

 HAYHOUSE RADIO
radio for your soul®

HealYourLife.com

Heal Your Life One Thought at a Time . . .
on Louise's All-New Website!

*"Life is bringing me everything
I need and more."*

— Louise Hay

Come to HEALYOURLIFE.COM today and meet the world's best-selling self-help authors; the most popular leading intuitive, health, and success experts; up-and-coming inspirational writers; and new like-minded friends who will share their insights, experiences, personal stories, and wisdom so you can heal your life and the world around you . . . one thought at a time.

Here are just some of the things you'll get at HealYourLife.com:

- DAILY AFFIRMATIONS
- CAPTIVATING VIDEO CLIPS
- EXCLUSIVE BOOK REVIEWS
- AUTHOR BLOGS
- LIVE TWITTER AND FACEBOOK FEEDS
- BEHIND-THE-SCENES SCOOPS
- LIVE STREAMING RADIO
- "MY LIFE" COMMUNITY OF FRIENDS

PLUS:
FREE Monthly Contests and Polls
FREE BONUS gifts, discounts, and newsletters

Make It Your Home Page Today!
www.HealYourLife.com®

HEAL YOUR LIFE♥